MW00714741

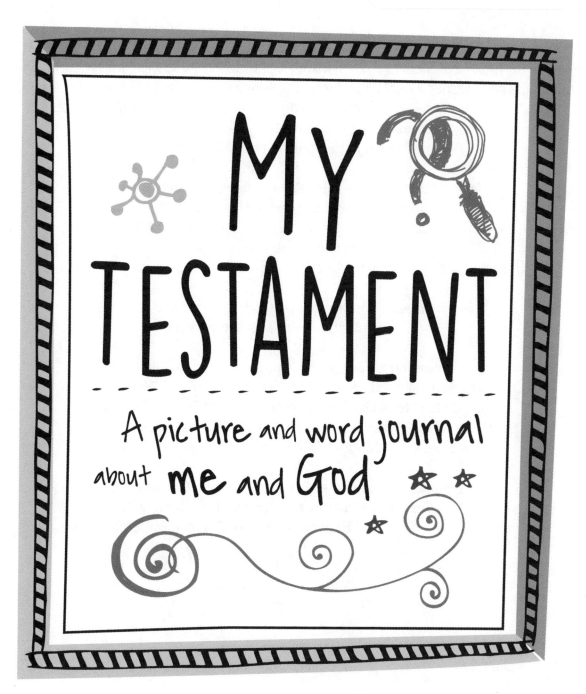

MY TESTAMENT

A picture and word journal about **me** and **God**

MARK BURROWS

MY TESTAMENT: A PICTURE AND WORD JOURNAL ABOUT ME AND GOD, STUDENT JOURNAL, VOLUME ONE. An official resource for The United Methodist Church approved by Discipleship Ministries (General Board of Discipleship) and published by Abingdon Press, a division of The United Methodist Publishing House, 2222 Rosa L. Parks Blvd., PO Box 280988, Nashville, TN 37228-0988. Price: $9.99.
Copyright © 2016 Abingdon Press. All rights reserved.
Printed in the United States of America.

To order copies of this publication, call toll free: 800-672-1789.
You may fax your order to 800-445-8189.
Telecommunication Device for the Deaf/Telex Telephone: 800-227-4091.
Or order online at *abingdonpress.com*.
Use your Cokesbury account, American Express, Visa, Discover, or MasterCard.

If you have questions or comments, call toll free: 800-672-1789.
Or e-mail *customerhelp@cokesbury.com*.

For information concerning permission to reproduce
any material in this publication, write to Rights and Permissions,
The United Methodist Publishing House, 2222 Rosa L. Parks Blvd.,
PO Box 280988, Nashville, TN 37228-0988. You may fax your request
to 615-749-6128. Or e-mail *permissions@umpublishing.org*.

Scripture quotations are from the Common English Bible.
Copyright © 2011 by the Common English Bible.
All rights reserved. Used by permission. *www.CommonEnglishBible.com*

16 17 18 19 20 21 22 23 24 25—10 9 8 7 6 5 4 3 2 1
ISBN: 9781501824166
PACP10492090-01

Editor: Nathan Tenney
Designer: Kellie Green

The Old Testament
is about…

The New Testament
is about…

_____

Testament is about my relationship with

God.

Something in God's creation I really like is...

The Creation

In the beginning God created the heavens and the earth.
On the first day God created day and night.
On the second day God created the firmament—the sky.
On the third day God created the land, the seas, and all the plant life that grows on land.
On the fourth day God created the sun, moon, and stars.
On the fifth day God created all the creatures of the sea and the birds of the air.
On the sixth day God created all the creatures on land, including people.
When God looked at all that God had made, God saw that it was good.
On the seventh day God rested and blessed the day as holy.
Based on Genesis 1:1–2:3.

Something in God's creation I don't like, but trust that God sees as good is...

**In the beginning was the Word and the Word was with God and the Word was God.
The Word was with God in the beginning.
John 1:1-2**

In the beginning, God knew that I would be.

God sees that I am good because...

Your thumbprint here

_____'s In-the-Beginning Moment

Your name here

Date:_____

Draw a tree that takes up the entire page.

Decorate the tree with the things that tempt you.

Then he went a short distance farther and fell on his face and prayed, "My Father, if it's possible, take this cup of suffering away from me. However—not what I want but what you want." Matthew 26:39

How will you choose to put God's way first?

Prayer

Draw a big cloud and fill it with any questions you have about the Noah story.
Leave room for raindrops.

Make a rainbow.

Write a note or prayer to God.

Abraham =

Sarah =

Isaac =

_____=_____
      your name

Peter =

Many Names of Jesus

God's Son—John 1:34
Human One—Luke 19:10
Word—John 1:1
Lamb—1 Corinthians 5:7
Deliverer—Romans 11:26
Cornerstone—Matthew 21:42
Leader and Savior—Acts 5:31
Teacher—John 20:16
Light of the World—John 8:12
Bread of Life—John 6:35
Gate of the Sheep—John 10:7
Good Shepherd—John 10:14
Prince of Peace—Isaiah 9:6
Emmanuel (God with us)—Matthew 1:23
Christ—Matthew 16:16
King—Luke 19:38
Messiah—John 4:25
True Vine—John 15:1

Five things I like about myself:

1.

2.

3.

4.

5.

Your name here

Three things I could do that would make God happy:

1.

2.

3.

My sacred nickname is:

What do you have a hard time believing or understanding (even if it's a Bible story)?

Remember, you can write or draw a picture...or *both*.

Jesus replied, "Do you believe because you see me?
Happy are those who don't see and yet believe."
John 20:29

I believe God:

I believe Jesus:

Faith is the reality of what we hope for, the proof of what we don't see.
Hebrews 11:1

You planned something bad for me, but God produced something good from it, in order to save the lives of many people, just as he's doing today.
Genesis 50:20

I believe in the sun even when it is not shining.
I believe in love even when I do not feel it.
I believe in God even when God is silent.

Completely color the page with colored pencil.
Use your pencil's eraser to write, *God's Plan*.

What is something irreplaceable you would save from your home in an emergency?

Draw a basket on the river, then draw that irreplaceable thing in the basket.

_____ , you are my child, whom I dearly love; in you I find happiness. —Based on Mark 1:11.

your first name

The Ten Commandments

1. No worshipping other gods.
2. No making or worshipping idols.
3. No misusing God's name.
4. Remember the sabbath day and keep it holy.
5. Respect your parents.
6. No killing.
7. Stay in love with the person you marry.
8. No stealing.
9. No telling lies about your neighbor.
10. No becoming jealous of your neighbor's stuff.

If you could make an 11th Commandment, what would it be?

What is the one rule at school you have the hardest time following?

What is a rule at home you have a hard time following?

Write or draw a short prayer to ask God for help following an important rule.

What qualities would you like a true friend to have?
Trace your left hand. List one quality in (or by) each finger.

**Wherever you go, I will go;
and wherever you stay, I will stay.
Your people will be my people,
and your God will be my God.
Ruth 1:16**

What qualities should you have?
Trace your right hand. List one quality in (or by) each finger.

Friends love all the time, and kinsfolk are born for times of trouble.
Proverbs 17:17

Fill this frame with words, pictures, or symbols to remind you of how God can help you.

Fill this space with something that scares you.

Write about or draw a picture of a situation that causes you stress or fear.

What is something you could do to help you remember that God's love is always with you?

**Don't be alarmed or terrified,
because the Lord your God is with you wherever you go.
Joshua 1:9**

The people walking in darkness have seen a great light.
On those living in a pitch-dark land, light has dawned.
Isaiah 9:2

The time is coming, declares the Lord,
when I will raise up a righteous descendant from David's line,
and he will rule as a wise king.
He will do what is just and right in the land.
Jeremiah 23:5

The Lord will give you a sign.
The young woman is pregnant and is about to give birth to a son,
and she will name him Immanuel.
Isaiah 7:14

A child is born to us, a son is given to us,
and authority will be on his shoulders.
He will be named
Wonderful Counselor, Mighty God, Eternal Father, Prince of Peace.
Isaiah 9:6

As for you, Bethlehem of Ephrathah, though you are the least significant of Judah's forces,
one who is to be a ruler in Israel on my behalf will come out from you.
His origin is from remote times, from ancient days.
Micah 5:2

What do you hope for yourself 20 years from now?

What do you hope for the world 20 years from now?

Create a Nativity scene.

Add words of hope (even bits of Scripture).

Trust in the Lord with all your heart; don't rely on your own intelligence.
Proverbs 3:5

Those who exploit the powerless anger their maker, while those who are kind to the poor honor God.
Proverbs 14:31

A sensitive answer turns back wrath, but an offensive word stirs up anger.
Proverbs 15:1

Better to be patient than a warrior,
and better to have self-control than to capture a city.
Proverbs 16:32

Friends love all the time, and kinsfolk are born for times of trouble.
Proverbs 17:17

Listen to advice and accept instruction, so you might grow wise in the future.
Proverbs 19:20

Even young people are known by their actions,
whether their conduct is pure and upright.
Proverbs 20:11

Acting with righteousness and justice is more valued by the Lord than sacrifice.
Proverbs 21:3

Let another person praise you, and not your own mouth; a stranger, and not your own lips.
Proverbs 27:2

Illustrate *you* living out one of the Proverbs.

What gift would you have brought to the Jesus child?
What would make that a wise gift?
Draw a picture of the gift.

Prayer

When I'm an adult, I want to be _____

Even young people are known by their actions,
whether their conduct is pure and upright.
Proverbs 20:11

Illustrate your superhero self.

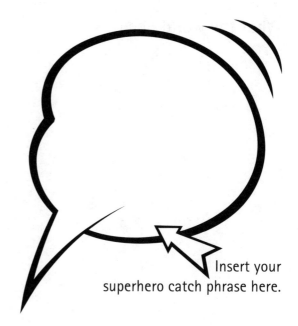

Insert your
superhero catch phrase here.

What the world needs:

What I care about:

Explore connections between the two lists. If you like, draw lines from one to the other.

I will follow Jesus because he is...

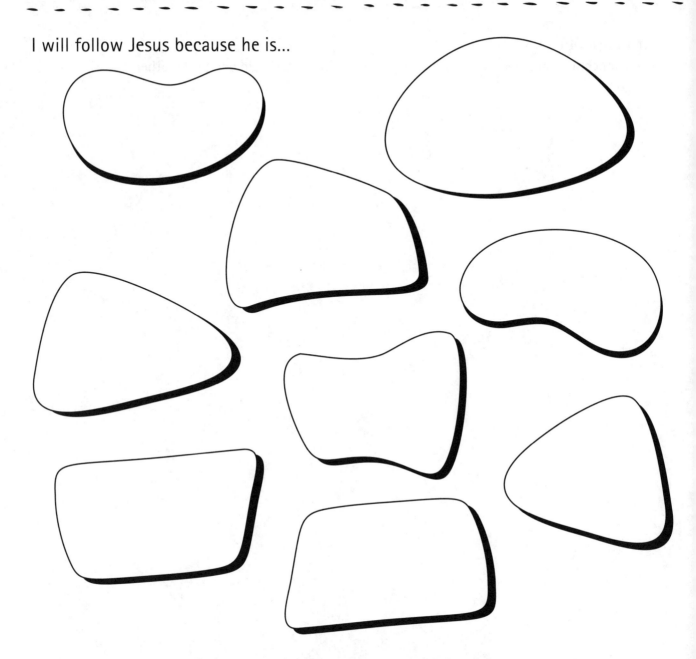

Christ has no body now on earth but yours,
no hands but yours, no feet but yours,
Yours are the eyes through which to look out
Christ's compassion to the world
Yours are the feet with which he is to go about doing good;
Yours are the hands with which he is to bless men now.
St. Teresa of Avila

What do you think God is calling you to do?
Write about it or draw a picture.

Who will stand with you?

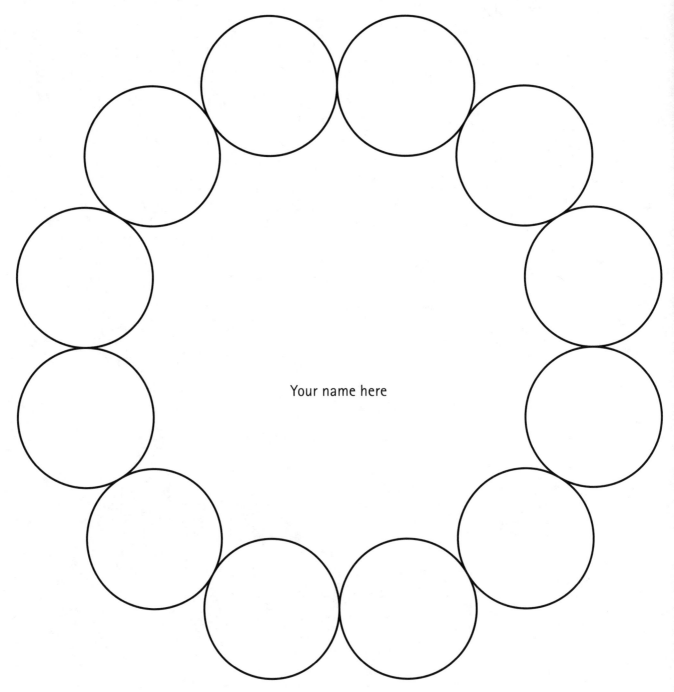

Your name here

Continue encouraging each other and building each other up.
1 Thessalonians 5:11

What do you think Jesus wrote in the dust?

God stood with _____

Jesus stood with _____

I will stand with _____

_____

+

_____

=

_____

Draw a person from Bible times.

What is something in our world today that this person might see as a miracle?

Prayer

What one food could you eat for 40 years?

What one thing could you drink for 40 years?

If I go 40 days without _____,
I know I will grow closer with God.

For 40 days, I will _____.

I'm landing punches on my own body and subduing it like a slave.
1 Corinthians 9:27

What is something you do or would like to do, but you're worried that others will think it's stupid?

Who's an authority figure you respect?
What's an activity that person might not have done since childhood?
Illustrate it.

How might that activity help that person glorify God?

When have you felt pressure to behave or talk a certain way so you wouldn't be left out?

Remember, you can write, draw a picture...or both.

Don't be conformed to the patterns of this world,
but be transformed by the renewing of your minds
so that you can figure out what God's will is—
what is good and pleasing and mature.
Romans 12:2

How could peer pressure be something positive?

Has anyone ever done or said something that made you so upset, you held on to feelings of resentment or anger?

Prayer

Mark out all of the negative words, leaving only the positive words.
Can any of the negative words be transformed?

Anger   Despair   Lies   Shoving
Mean   Words   Hateful   Punching
Hopeless   God   Faithless   Lost
Never   Unloved   Shines   Woe
Hostility   Intolerance   Bitter
Greed   Light   Hurting   Crying   Pain
Kicking   Stormy   Jealous   Fear
Friendless   Spiteful   Life   Envious
Yelling   Blame   Biting   Sadness
Gossip   Love   Shame   Mocking
Impossible   Doubt   Wrong

My hometown:

What I love about my hometown:

One thing I would change about my hometown:

Write your name vertically in BIG letters.

Use each letter in your name as the first letter of a good quality you have.

Prayer

The LORD is my shepherd.
I lack nothing.

He lets me rest in grassy meadows;
he leads me to restful waters;

he keeps me alive.
He guides me in proper paths
for the sake of his good name.

Even when I walk through the darkest valley,
I fear no danger because you are with me.
Your rod and your staff—
they protect me.

You set a table for me
right in front of my enemies.
You bathe my head in oil;
my cup is so full it spills over!

Yes, goodness and faithful love
will pursue me all the days of my life,
and I will live in the LORD's house
as long as I live.
Psalm 23

Name a song that comforts you.

Why do you reject my very being, Lord?
Why do you hide your face from me?

Since I was young I've been afflicted, I've been dying.
I've endured your terrors. I'm lifeless.

Your fiery anger has overwhelmed me; your terrors have destroyed me.

They surround me all day long like water; they engulf me completely.

You've made my loved ones and companions distant.
My only friend is darkness.
Psalm 88:14-18

Name a sad song or movie that you like.

Shout triumphantly to the Lord, all the earth!

Serve the Lord with celebration!
Come before him with shouts of joy!

Know that the Lord is God—he made us; we belong to him.
We are his people, the sheep of his own pasture.

Enter his gates with thanks; enter his courtyards with praise!
Thank him! Bless his name!

Because the Lord is good, his loyal love lasts forever;
his faithfulness lasts generation after generation.
Psalm 100

Name a song that really makes you happy.

Love is patient, love is kind, it isn't jealous, it doesn't brag,
it isn't arrogant, it isn't rude, it doesn't seek its own advantage,
it isn't irritable, it doesn't keep a record of complaints,
it isn't happy with injustice, but it is happy with the truth.
Love puts up with all things, trusts in all things,
hopes for all things, endures all things.

Love never fails.
As for prophecies, they will be brought to an end.
As for tongues, they will stop.
As for knowledge, it will be brought to an end.
1 Corinthians 13:4-8

I can endure all these things through the power of the one who gives me strength.
Philippians 4:13

Rejoice always. Pray continually.
1 Thessalonians 5:16-17

Write a letter to a person or people in a specific place, encouraging them in the faith.

**In fact, if you don't speak up at this very important time,
relief and rescue will appear for the Jews from another place,
but you and your family will die. But who knows?
Maybe it was for a moment like this
that you came to be part of the royal family.
Esther 4:14**

When have you been in the right place at the right time?

There's a season for everything
and a time for every matter under the heavens:
a time for giving birth and a time for dying,
a time for planting and a time for uprooting what was planted,
a time for killing and a time for healing,
a time for tearing down and a time for building up,
a time for crying and a time for laughing,
a time for mourning and a time for dancing,
a time for throwing stones and a time for gathering stones,
a time for embracing and a time for avoiding embraces,
a time for searching and a time for losing,
a time for keeping and a time for throwing away,
a time for tearing and a time for repairing,
a time for keeping silent and a time for speaking,
a time for loving and a time for hating,
a time for war and a time for peace.
Ecclesiastes 3:1-8

How can you spend *time* being attentive to others?

What about God or God's world makes you say, "Wow!"?

Wow

Create an "I'm Sorry" prayer, confessing something you know you've done wrong.

I'm Sorry

Write a thank-you note to God for some blessing in your life.

Thank
You

Ask God for help with something, or for someone else.

Help

What country would you like to visit and why?

What is a language you would like to learn?

What is your favorite kind of food from a culture other than your own?

Peace in Many Languages

Peace	English
Paz	Spanish
Shalom	Hebrew
Salaam	Arabic
Frieden	German
Amani	Swahili
Heiwa	Japanese
Mir	Russian
Maluhia	Hawaiian
Pyonghwa	Korean

Prayer

Fill this page with symbols of peace, or draw what you imagine a peaceful world would look like.

Come, Holy Spirit. Help me see God's love in others. Help me seek to understand. Amen.